CRAWLEY
The Making of a New Town

Grand Parade, Crawley High Street, erected in the late 1930s as the town's first 'purpose-built' row of shops.

CRAWLEY

The Making of a New Town

Roger Bastable

Phillimore

1986

Published by
PHILLIMORE & CO. LTD.
Shopwyke Hall, Chichester, Sussex

ISBN 0 85033 613 9

Printed and bound in Great Britain by
BIDDLES LTD.
Guildford, Surrey

To the lifelong friends I met while studying History
at the University of Newcastle Upon Tyne, 1969-1972

Contents

List of Illustrations

Acknowledgements

In common with, I am sure, most compilers of Pictorial Histories, I must start with a general acknowledgement of all those who have been prepared to lend me photographs, without which this book would never have materialised. Yet again, I have been amazed at the generosity and trust of people in and around Crawley who have been willing to allow me not only to look at their treasured photographs and documents, but also to take material away to be copied. I hope that this book will justify all the help and encouragement I have been given.

The majority of photographs included here have been copied from the large collection in Crawley Library, and I gratefully acknowledge the kindness of the County Library Service in allowing their reproduction. As before I must record special thanks to Mr. Charles Kay of Crawley Library, who has been of inestimable help in my research, with his knowledge, advice, and above all his unfailing courtesy and patience. I should also like to acknowledge the help and support given to me by Mrs. Polly Massé, who has allowed me unrestricted access to the excellent photographic collection of her late husband, Harry. As well as collecting old photographs of Crawley, many of which I had not seen before, he also had the foresight in the early to mid-1950s to photograph streets and buildings which he knew would soon be demolished, and Parts 3 and 4 draw extensively on his collection. Finally, I must also record particular thanks to Mr. Les Collins, not only for lending me his fine sepia prints of the Imperial cinema for inclusion in this book, but especially for a fascinating morning in April 1986, when he took me on a 'guided tour' of what remains of the Imperial today.

It will become apparent that I have a particular interest in the history of the Crabbet Park Estate, an interest which grew out of my mention of Crabbet in *Crawley - A Pictorial History*. Thanks to the co-operation and kindness of Mr. Ken Boyle and the staff of Stiles, Horton & Ledger of Crawley, I have since embarked on some extensive research on the history of the estate, which I hope to make the subject of another photographic compilation in the near future. My research introduced me in the autumn of 1984 to Lady Winifrid Tryon, younger daughter of Lady Wentworth and the Hon. Neville Lytton, later 3rd Earl of Lytton, of Crabbet Park. Lady Winifrid sadly died in May 1985, at the age of 81, yet before her death she showed a great keenness that the history of Crabbet be recorded, and it was she who kindly lent me some of the photographs of Crabbet Park House and of her mother, Lady Wentworth, which have been reproduced in this book. I also gratefully acknowledge the present owner of the photographs, Lady Lucy Lytton, for permission to include them.

I should like to thank Sir Norman and Lady Longley for allowing me to borrow photographs from the book commemorating the first hundred years that the firm of James Longley has been part of Crawley life; no history of Crawley would be complete without reference to its most famous construction company. I also gratefully acknowledge the help I have received from those who have allowed me to borrow and reproduce photographs for this book: Mr. Rod Balkham, Barbara and Norman Barnard, Miss Cis Briggs, Mrs. Margaret Butler, Mr. Bob Cooper, Mr. Bert Croyden, Mrs. Gret Cureton, Miss Irene Dennis, Mr. Peter Gwynne, Chairman of the Crawley Museum Society, Mrs. Elsie Hillier, Mrs. Frances Hogger, Mrs. Gwen Hooker, Mr. Lanaway, Mrs. Lily Langridge, Mr. Ernie Matthews, Mr. Jack Norman, Miss Betty Pedder, Mrs. Jean Riley, Mr. Michael Sadler, Mr. Jim Stephenson, Manager of the *George Hotel*, Mr. George Surridge, Mrs. Mavis Thomas, Mr. T. J. Thomas, Headmaster of St. Margaret's School, Ifield, Miss Tickner, Miss Diana Veitch, Mrs. Percy Wales, and Mrs. Amy Wilson. I gratefully acknowledge the Ordnance Survey Office and Commission for the New Towns for allowing me to reproduce material.

I should also like to thank my cousin, Sue Quinn, for sorting out my original text and retyping it for me, correctly spelt and punctuated. Of all my many friends and colleagues who have given me so much encouragement, I should like to thank especially Leslie Coate for his professional criticism and advice, and Mary Cheadle of Holy Trinity School, Crawley for her patience and forebearance. Most of all, I should like to record my heartfelt appreciation and gratitude to my parents, not just for their customary encouragement, but for their love and support in a year which has been fraught for them as well as for me.

Introduction

'Crawley's story is our story ... not just of our town, nor only of those who have made it their home for generations, but the story of the human instinct to survive, grow and prosper ... ' Each evening during the third week of June 1986, these words introduced the *Son et Lumière* production, which told the story of Crawley from its humble Saxon beginnings until the present day. It became the main event of the Crawley Festival, organised to celebrate and commemorate the approaching fortieth anniversary of Crawley's designation as a New Town.

This second volume of photographs focuses on the last hundred years in the story of a town unique in the social and economic history of Britain; certainly, no great historical events took place here, nor has any famous historical personage made it his home. Yet the story of the Saxon clearing, named 'Crow lea' or Crawley, is the story of man himself. These photographs show how Crawley has reacted to the great events of history, significantly the two World Wars, the transport revolutions, and the establishment of a planned community.

My first volume, *Crawley - A Pictorial History*, published in 1983, concentrated on the history of Crawley from a geographical and thematic point of view. *Crawley - The Making of a New Town* is more chronological in layout. Divided into four parts, it reveals the changing face of the town from the 1880s, when Crawley was beginning to expand, to the 1980s, when it has a population in excess of 80,000 and the reputation of being one of the most prosperous regions in Britain.

There are two reasons for concentrating on the last hundred years in the history of a town whose origins go back a thousand years; the first, and most obvious of course, that the invention of the camera in the last century and the resulting fund of photographic material have made it far easier to compile a pictorial record of that time. The second reason is that the last hundred years have witnessed more significant change than any comparable period in history, and that within this time, Crawley has been subject to more development than most towns of similar size and character.

The sub-title of this book 'The Making of a New Town' does not just refer to the last forty years, although the designation of Crawley as a New Town in 1947 and the coming to fruition of the original plans forms a suitable climax. However, as early as 1886, there were signs that Crawley was expanding rapidly. The rise in Crawley's population from the middle of the century, following the coming of the railway, resulted in a wave of urban development, part of which became known as early as 1870 as 'New Town'. Similarly, the two Worlds Wars had a devastating effect on Crawley, all but destroying by 1950 the close, tight pattern of small-town society once believed to be as indestructible as the British Empire itself. One fascinating clue to the shifting social trends since 1886 can be detected in the rise and fall of the landed estate. 'From Country Estate To Housing Estate' could be an alternative sub-title to this book, since Crawley provides a near 'text book' example of the social revolution of the last fifty years. As a gauge to this gradual, then rapid social shift, each part of the book features photographs of the Crabbet Park Estate, one of the many which had encircled Crawley in 1886. A century later it has, like its immediate neighbours, been divided into many parts.

To conclude, my aim in compiling this second volume of 'old Crawley' photographs has been twofold; firstly, that the great social changes of the last hundred years can be seen and understood within the context of one town; and secondly the hope that by discovering Crawley's roots, its inhabitants will be able to regard the town with the pride and affection it deserves as they look to its future. I shall not see the publication of *Crawley - A Pictorial History 1986-2086*, but hope it will be as fascinating a story as that of the last hundred years.

Roger Bastable
CRAWLEY, June 1986

Part One: 1886-1910

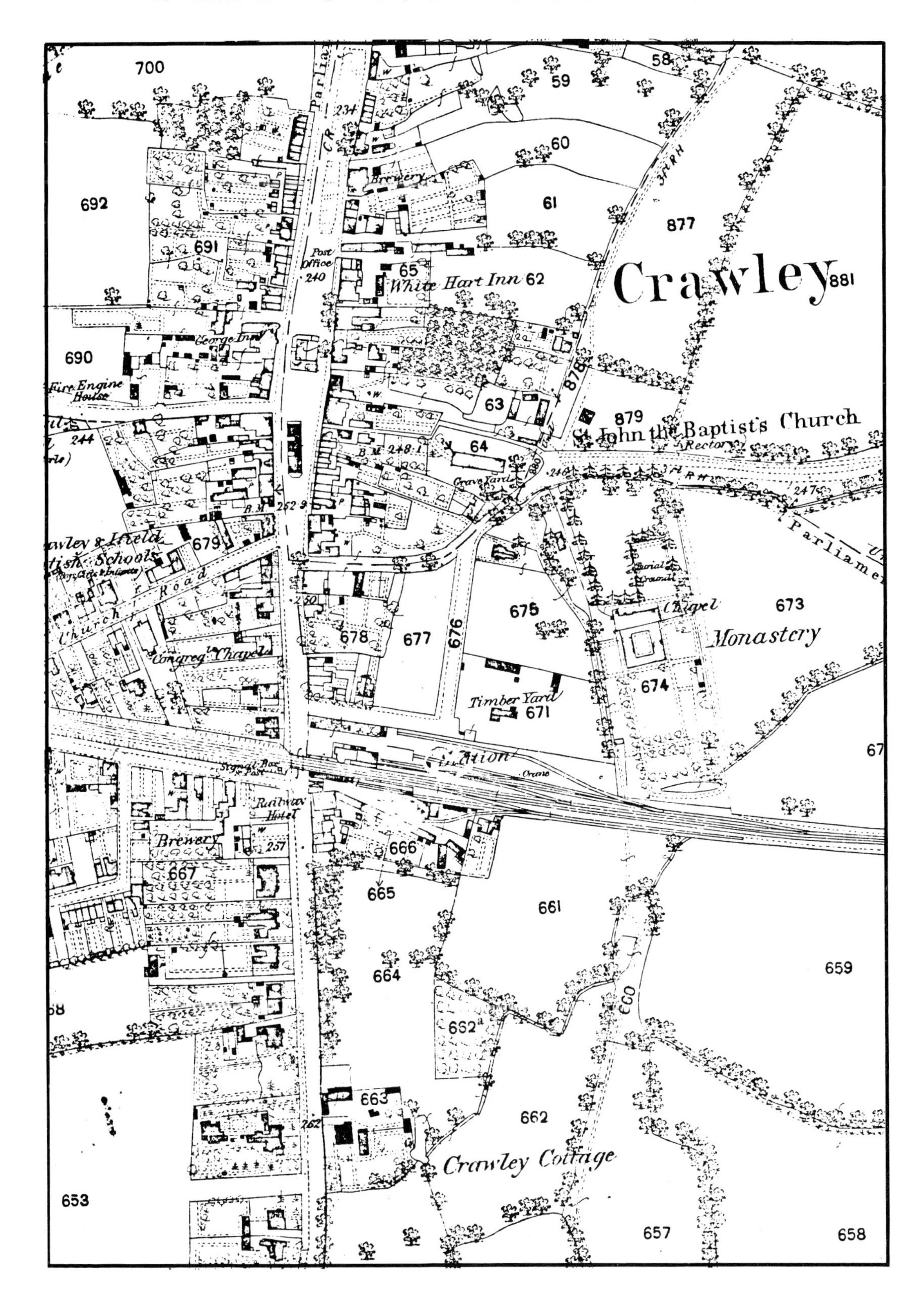

1. (*previous page*) A map of Crawley in the 1870s, with the small town based around the High Street, as it had been since the first turnpike from Crawley to Reigate was opened in the 1690s. This is a particularly interesting map since a number of buildings are labelled, such as the *George Inn* and the *White Hart*, built in 1790 to cope with the rapid increase of passing coaches. By 1870 there were signs of change. There had been fears that the construction by the London, Brighton & South Coast Railway Co. of a main line from London Bridge through Three Bridges would condemn Crawley to a future of mouldering obscurity. In fact, however, the extension of a branch line from Three Bridges to Horsham in 1848 instigated a wave of expansion, evident by the time that this map was printed.

The villages of Crawley and Ifield were sufficiently developed to provide two schools (the National School, 1825, and the British School, 1854), some time before elementary education was made compulsory; likewise, by 1870, Crawley was able to offer alternatives to the Anglican parish church of St John the Baptist, with the Bethel Chapel (1856), the Congregational church (1862), the Roman Catholic Franciscan Friary (1861), and the Baptist church (1883), quite remarkable for a small country town.

Perhaps the most interesting and significant aspect of this map is the building of a small housing development to the west of the railway station, known as 'New Town'. The years immediately after the coming of the railway to Crawley saw a rapid rise in population and the establishment of small firms, which were able to offer employment other than agricultural work. One such firm was that of Richard Cook, who set up his builder's yard along the railway line, and who built the small development of 'New Town', comprising mainly West Street, which still stands in 1986 as a reminder of Crawley's first planned urban development. Within a few years, 'New Town' was to be matched by a similar, even larger, development to the east, with the arrival of James Longley, whose building and joinery business was established alongside the railway line, where it still stands today.

CRAWLEY is a parish and pleasant village, a great portion of which stands in Ifield parish, on the Horsham branch of the London, Brighton and South Ceast line of railway, 1 mile from the Three Bridges station, 30½ miles from London, 7 from Horsham, and 9½ north from Cuckfield, in Bottinghill hundred, East Grinstead union, rape, archdeaconry and deanery of Lewes, East Sussex, diocese of Chichester, and county court district of Horsham. The population of Crawley is 447, but including the Ifield side it is more than 1,000; the area is 770 acres. The church of St. John the Baptist is an old stone building, with nave, chancel and square tower. The register dates from 1658. The living is a rectory, value £98 yearly, with residence, in the gift of Lieut.-Gen. Clitherow, and held by the Rev. John Soper, B.A., of Magdalen Hall, Oxford. Here are chapels for Independents and Baptists, and a National and a British school. A Roman Catholic church was erected in 1861, at a cost of upwards of £2,000; it is a brick and stone building, dedicated to St. Francis; the Rev. Father Anthony is priest. The village has recently been lighted with gas, and it contains some good and well-filled shops, and two good Inns. There are fairs for horses and cattle on the 8th of May and 9th of September, and a corn market every Wednesday evening, at the 'White Hart.' About a mile north stood the county oak, at the Surrey boundary, on Lowfield Heath.

Broadwood John, esq. Buchan hill
Browne Mr. Peter Agate, Crawley villa
Caffin Mr. Joseph Matthws. Clifton villa
Callyn Mr. Richard
Dempster Mrs
Gates Mr. William
Girling Mrs. Crawley villa
Lemon Mark, esq. Vine cottage
Norton Misses
Norton Mr. Theodore
Power Rev. Anthony
Smith Thomas, esq
Soper Rev. John, B.A. Rectory
Tusler Mr. James, Perry cottage
Verey Mrs
Wood Mr. Peter

COMMERCIAL.

Andrews Joseph, tinman
Bisshopp Cecil, plumber & glazier
Bowers Stephen, shoemaker
Bowers William, boot & shoe maker
Branch Melancthon, wheelwright
Bridger Henry, mealman
Bridger Richard, beer retailer
Budgen John, cooper, West green
Callyn John, butcher
Cutler John, auctioneer & appraiser, Springfield
Foster Joseph, chimney sweeper
Gasson Marian Harriet (Miss), milliner
Gates Charles, grocer
Gates Stephen, carpenter
Gates Robert & Richard, builders
Gravely Thomas, baker
Heathfield John, blacksmith
Hobbs John, baker
Hollman & Bowers, bootmakers & leather cutters
Humphrey & Son, blacksmiths
Knight John, tailor & stationer
Leach John, chemist & dentist
Lillywhite Thomas, tailor
Little & Sons, drapers & grocers
Miller Nathaniel, saddler & harness mkr
Mitchell James, watchmaker
Mitchell William, stationer
Morley Joseph, millwright
Nightingale William, brick & tile maker
Ockenden Charles, *George hotel, commercial inn & posting house*
Ockenden George, tailor & hatter
Ockenden Hen. & Son, builders, West grn
Packham Henry, wheelwright
Pickett James, patten & clog maker
Reeves Caleb, watchmaker
Robinson John, farmer, Manor farm
Russell Fredk. hairdresser & bird stuffer
Russell Louisa (Mrs.), shopkeeper
Sayers Edward, beer retailer & blacksmith, West green
Simmins Wm. corn, coal & lime merchant, dealer in artificial manure, & agent for Thorley's cattle food, Railway station
Smith & Son, grocers, drapers & millers
Smith Thomas, surgeon
Snelling Louis, shopkeeper, West green
Soan Harry & Thos. plumbers, painters & glaziers
Stone Stephen, shopkeeper, West green
Tyler William, *White Hart*
Wales Ephraim, builder, West green
Webley Ambose, *Station inn*, & licensed to let horses
Wood Amos, shopkeeper
Worsfold & Son, blacksmiths
Wright John, butcher

POST OFFICE & POST OFFICE SAVINGS BANK.—Wm. Mitchell, postmaster. Letters from London arrive at 2 & 11.15 a.m.; dispatched at 2.5 & 10.40 p.m. Money orders are granted & paid at this office

INSURANCE AGENTS:—
County Fire, James Tusler
Edinburgh Life, John Knight
Phœnix Fire, John Knight
Provident Life, James Tusler
Royal Fire & Life, William Simmins
Temperance General & Provident, John Sayers

Gasworks, Thos. Smith, esq. treasurer; Mr. Ambrose Webley & Mr. J. M. Caffin, managing directors; John Sayers, sec
Railway Station, William Simmins, station master
Parish Clerk, James Still

PUBLIC SCHOOLS:—
British (for boys & girls), John Sayers, master
Infant, Miss Ann Deadman, mistress
National, James Gibb, master; Mrs. Jane Gibb, mistress

POSTING HOUSE.—*George hotel*, Charles Ockenden

2. The entry for Crawley in Pigot's *Directory* of the time shows a well-ordered society, with everybody knowing his or her place. Far from causing resentment, such a hierarchy spelt order and stability for all from the local squire down to the humble shopkeeper and blacksmith.

3. Crawley Green, looking northwards, in a photograph dating from about 1889. The old village green was at this time set well back from the High Street, with the buildings, fortunately still standing in 1986, which date from the Middle Ages—the 'Tree House' in the distance, home of the Smith family, with the medieval farmhouse, later to become *Ye Olde Punch Bowle* and then the National Westminster Bank. When this photograph was taken the old farmhouse was divided into two small farmworkers' cottages.

4. A delightful, though sadly faded, rural scene, dating from about 1880, and barely recognisable today. This must have been Crawley as countless road travellers would have first seen it, having passed through the north tollgate, and with the street widening out in the distance with the *White Hart* to the left and the *George* to the right. Unfortunately, most of the houses in this picture, many of which dated from before the 16th century, no longer exist.

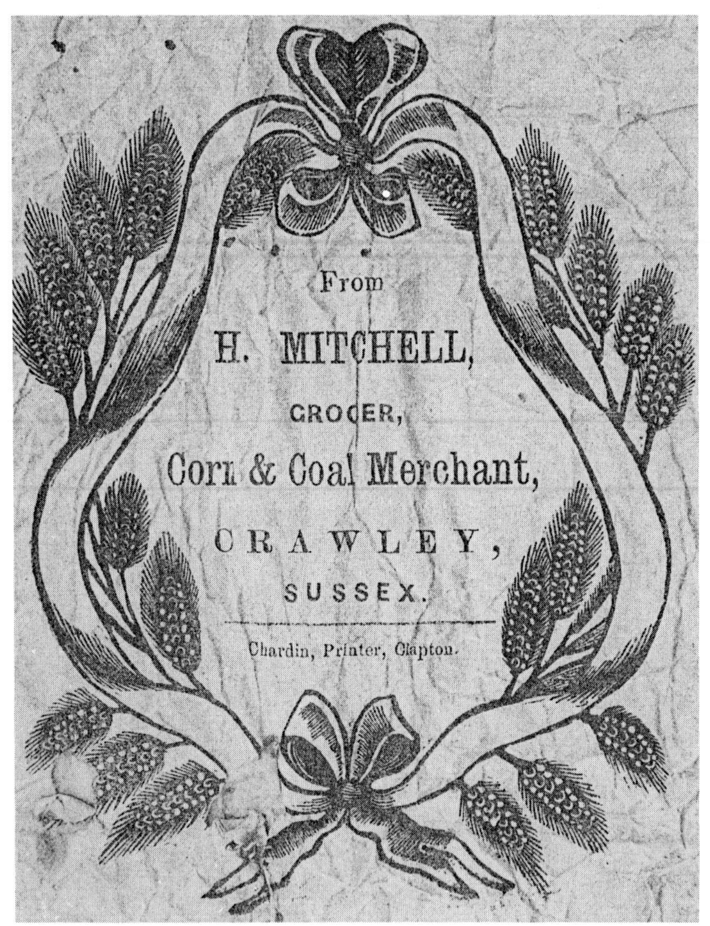

5. (*above*) The *White Hart Inn*, photographed at the turn of the century. Built in 1790 to accommodate the vast increase in coach traffic, it replaced the original *White Hart* opposite the *George*, now *Solomon's Ancient Priors*, and haunt of smugglers in the 18th century. The new *White Hart*, a purpose-built coaching inn, not dissimilar to the modern motorway motel, conducted a far more reputable line of business: as well as dispensing refreshment and accommodation for man and horse alike, it was from 1810 until 1895 the site of Crawley's post office.

6. (*left*) One notable feature of late 19th-century Crawley, as with any small town or village of the time, was the family business, reflecting the solidity of the social structure and the limitations of travel. For long a cornerstone of Victorian small town society, the family business flourished in many crafts and professions, often making a name synonymous with a particular line of business. One such name in Crawley was that of Mitchell, associated primarily with the post office. William Mitchell was Crawley's first postmaster (a position held by the landlord of the *White Hart* from 1810 to 1828) and was followed by his son Charles, until his retirement in 1908. This is part of what must be one of Crawley's oldest surviving paper bags, from the Grocer, Corn and Coal Merchant's business of Charles's brother Horatio, whose shop (in the front parlour of his Regency house) was one of Crawley's first.

7. An unusual photograph of St John's parish church, in about 1869, during the time of Revd. John Soper, and showing its appearance before the extensive alterations carried out by Soper's successor, the energetic John Barrett-Lennard. The church had undergone little alteration since the 15th century and practically none since the tower was extended in 1804.

8. The interior of St John's at the turn of the century, looking towards the recently remodelled chancel; most of the Victorian alterations were made at Barrett-Lennard's instigation, and the rector himself was responsible for much of the intricate wood-carving in the choir stalls, including the rector's chair, with the words 'Lord, Teach Us to Pray'. Ever mindful of his congregation, he had carved into the 17th-century pulpit, within sight of the preacher, 'Be Brief'.

9. St John's choir in the 1880s.

1879

CRAWLEY CHURCH RESTORATION BAZAAR.

Extracts collected from the "Sussex Daily News," of the Bazaar proceedings, held on the Rectory Grounds, Thursday and Friday, July 17th and 18th.

Friday, 18th July.

"CHURCH BAZAAR.—A grand bazaar in aid of the church restoration funds was held yesterday in the Rectory Grounds. From an early hour flags and bunting of various sorts were exhibited in profusion, particularly about the Railway Station—the work of the worthy Stationmaster —and also in that part of the town approaching the Rectory Grounds. In the grounds themselves, a great variety of ensigns lent a charm to the scene; also on the steeple of the church the Union Jack was conspicuous. The weather although threatening in the early part of the day, with a slight rain, improved as the day wore on. The Bazaar opened at two o'clock, from which hour the *élite* of the neighbourhood and from a distance were to be seen patronising the various stalls. These had been lib-

10. Part of a local newspaper account of the 'Church Restoration Bazaar' held in the Rectory grounds in July 1879. The Rectory and grounds have now been engulfed by the offices and shops of Crawley's busy Boulevard. John Barrett-Lennard, 'J. B.' as he was affectionately known in the parish, was rector of Crawley from 1876-98. He was the driving force behind much of the rebuilding undertaken at St John's during the 1880s.

11. One of the earliest photographs of Crawley's level crossing in the High Street, dating from about 1885. The opening of the Three Bridges-Horsham branch line through Crawley in 1848 marked the beginning of the town's Victorian development, although the land surrounding the railway was still largely open country. In the photograph can be seen the premises of Moses Nightingale, 'Corn Dealer & Seed Merchant', on the corner of Brighton Road.

12. The master and staff of Crawley railway station in the early 1890s, with the signal box, *Railway Hotel* and assembly rooms to the left, overlooking the west-bound platform.

13. The map of Crawley in the 1870s (*see* plate 1) shows the beginning of housing development adjacent to the station, which was known as 'New Town'. This photograph from the 1880s shows the junction of what is now Springfield Road and West Street. The man responsible for the development of Crawley's Victorian 'New Town' was Richard Cook, whose builder's yard can be seen to the right. This comparatively unknown photograph indicates that urban development in Crawley belongs by no means exclusively to the 20th century.

14. Unlike the housing developments of the 1980s, Richard Cook's 'New Town' stood within yards of the High Street, as it still does over a century later. This photograph shows the charming Victorian terraced houses and villas as they appear today; although many have been extensively modernised inside, their exterior still retains a Victorian flavour.

15. A gang of Richard Cook's workers.

16. Although Station Road had been laid out in the 1870s map of Crawley, it was yet to be developed; however, within a short space of time, this area between St John's church and the station housed detached and semi-detached villas, including Crawley's first police station.

17. Like 'New Town' and West Street, another part of Victorian Crawley to have survived into the 1980s is the residential development to the east of the High Street, running adjacent to the railway line, and contained in East Park and Malthouse Road. Both this photograph and plate 18 have no need of modern comparisons, since they look much the same today. Unlike West Street, East Park was built on a slightly grander scale with a profusion of detached and semi-detached villas.

18. Malthouse Road, which leads off from East Park, remains an interesting slice of late 19th-century social history, starting at one end with terraced cottages, progressing to semi-detached and detached houses. At the point where this photograph was taken the semi-detached houses give way to substantial villas in their own grounds. The main difference between these pictures and the same streets today is the almost continuous line of parked cars.

Steam Joinery Works.
Crawley, Sussex.

M

To James Longley & Co. Ltd.
Builders and Contractors.
Manufacturers of Longley's Improved System of Wood Block Flooring.
Prices on application.

19. Without doubt the best-known firm of Crawley builders remains that of James Longley, largely responsible for the building of Malthouse Road, as well as Longley's own house 'The Beeches', which still stands at the end of East Park, alongside the original 'steam joinery works'. This distinguished bust is of James Longley, the firm's founder, who moved his company to Crawley from Turners Hill in 1881, at the very time that the once small coaching town was beginning to expand.

20. On arriving in Crawley in the early 1880s, James Longley's company set about constructing Sussex's first steam-powered joinery works; the tall chimney, part of which can be seen in this photograph of about 1882, still stands, over a century later.

21. & 22. Crawley commemorated Queen Victoria's Golden Jubilee in June 1887 by planting an oak sapling on the Green, now, almost a century later, a huge tree. The town turned out in force again 10 years later to celebrate the Diamond Jubilee, which Crawley marked in a variety of ways: a sedate children's party in the garden of Mr. Moses Nightingale's home 'Hazeldene' (plate 21, *above*) and a rather more lusty gathering of the town's schoolchildren, watched by what appears to be most of the local population, in front of the railway station (plate 22, *below left*).

23. The Assembly Room Concert Party had become an integral part of Victorian Crawley's celebrations.

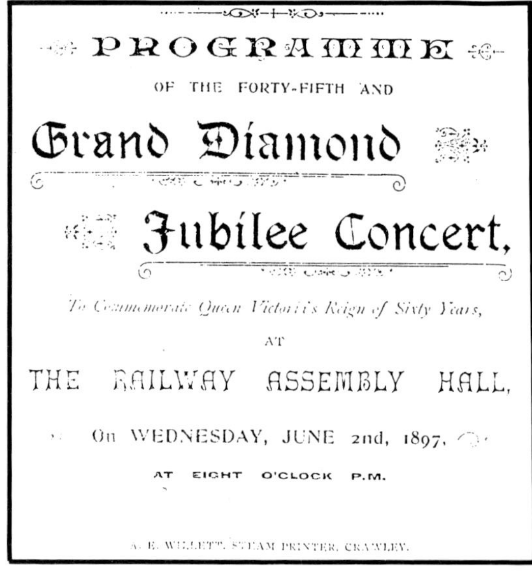

PROGRAMME

OF THE FORTY-FIFTH AND

Grand Diamond

Jubilee Concert,

To Commemorate Queen Victoria's Reign of Sixty Years,

AT

THE RAILWAY ASSEMBLY HALL,

On WEDNESDAY, JUNE 2nd, 1897,

AT EIGHT O'CLOCK P.M.

A. E. WILLETT, STEAM PRINTER, CRAWLEY.

24. This photograph of Crawley High Street, otherwise known as the Square, dating from the turn of the century looks northwards towards the village green; notice how the Jubilee Oak (1887) has grown.

25. The east side of the Square. This photograph, taken at about the same time as the one above, shows the old 'Priest's House' in a rather sorry state of repair, looking unusually deserted with a 'To Let' sign over the door. Until 1916, the building, which had once been the home of the famous Sussex ironmaster, Leonard Gale, belonged to the Crabbet Park Estate, owned by the Blunt family, descended from Gale's grand-daughter Sarah.

26. On the 1870s map what is known today as Robinson Road, just off the High Street, was marked as Church Road. This must be one of the few roads in Crawley to change its name four times; originally christened New Road, the establishment of two chapels by 1870 turned it into Church Road, until the post office was built there in 1895, when it became Post Office Road. It was only when the post office moved to new premises in the High Street in 1928 that it was given its present name in honour of Mrs. Sarah Robinson who founded the British School here in 1854. It can be seen to the left opposite the post office. This once very busy Victorian street, which housed two chapels, a school, post office and cottage hospital (to the immediate left), apart from a number of cottages and villas, is today sadly deserted, with many of its buildings demolished.

27. At the far end of Post Office Road stood 'Oak Lodge', which was the home of Crawley's famous postmaster, Mr. Charles Mitchell from the time of his retirement in 1908. By then, Crawley post office had been in the capable hands of the Mitchell family for 80 years so Charles' retirement justified a special evening's entertainment and a presentation at 'Hazeldene', the home of Moses Nightingale.

28. A drawing of the British School, Post Office Road, founded in 1854 thanks to subscriptions raised by Mrs. Sarah Robinson of Manor Farm, County Oak.

29. One of the young classes at the British School, posing for their group photograph in 1908.

30. By the turn of the century, Crawley had grown considerably. From the building of the railway in the 1840s until the 1880s, this part of Crawley High Street was entirely residential, but by the end of Victoria's reign, what had once been quietly-shaded gardens were now built on for shop premises, such as 'Vine Cottage' to the right of the picture, with Wilson's the grocers, Harry Charman, outfitter, and the International Stores.

31. The complacency of the Victorian age was to receive a jolt with the South African (Boer) War of 1899-1902, which marked a serious challenge to British Imperial rule in Africa. One of the many local men who volunteered to fight and embarked for South Africa was Lance-Corporal Frank Cooper from West Green, who served in the 2nd V.B. Royal Sussex Regiment.

32. Apart from the shops themselves, very little has altered in the eighty or so years since this photograph was taken at the junction of Brighton Road and East Park.

33. This photograph, taken from the same spot, looks to the opposite side of the road, showing the railway crossing gates, the castellated 'London & County Bank', and 'Gadsdon's' garage alongside. It was taken in July 1908 on the occasion of the visit of Princess Alexander of Teck.

34., 35. & 36. West Green, about a quarter of a mile from Crawley along the Ifield Road, had medieval origins but remained a small hamlet until the mid-19th century, when it was extensively developed, practically amalgamating with Crawley. Again, surprisingly little has changed since these pictures were taken in the 1900s. One of the oldest buildings seen in these views of Edwardian West Green was the National School (seen to the far right of plate 34), founded by Mrs. Sarah Robinson in 1825. It was the recalcitrance of the vicar of Ifield which led her to raise subscriptions for the British School in 1854. By the turn of the century, the National School had become West Green Church of England School; although the building survived the removal of the school to Ifield in 1955, it has been so altered as to be unrecognisable today.

37. An early class photograph from West Green School, with Mr. Wilton, the headmaster.

38. An older, apparently hard-working class at West Green, in about 1914. It is interesting to see how boys and girls are carefully segregated in the classroom as well as the playground.

39. The heart of old West Green was a cluster of cottages, with a small green in the centre: the traditional medieval pattern, and similar to Ifield, although on a much smaller scale. For centuries, West Green, along with the west side of Crawley High Street, lay in the parish of Ifield. West Green's own church was that of St Mary Magdalene, Alpha Road, until the larger church of St Peter's was erected on the village green in 1892. Apart from the demolition of some cottages in the distance, again very little has changed and West Green still retains its village atmosphere.

40. An early photograph of the interior of St Peter's, West Green, designed on late Victorian High Anglican lines.

41. An interesting, if rather stilted, postcard view of Crawley railway crossing in about 1910; the absence of traffic and willingness of people to stand in the road are more dated than the buildings themselves.

42. One of the most charming rows of cottages in Crawley High Street (demolished in the 1930s to make way for Grand Parade) forms the background for the London to Brighton Stock Exchange Walk of 1903. Unfortunately none of these buildings survive today.

43. By the reign of Edward VII the motor vehicle had become a familiar sight on Crawley's roads, especially as the town still formed part of the main London to Brighton road, although the old turnpike system had long since disappeared. Only a few miles north of Crawley is the village of Handcross where the Vanguard motor accident took place in July 1906, resulting in some fatalities; it seems strange that this incident should be commemorated on this postcard, now badly damaged.

44. One of Crawley's earliest football teams, photographed around 1895.

45. Another 'team' was the Crawley Town Band, seen here in pre-1914 days setting out for a concert or competition in one of Mr. Gadsdon's charabancs.

46. The Crawley Town Prize Band proudly posing with their instruments and newly-won trophy in 1906.

47. & 48. One of the most distinctive features of Crawley High Street in the opening years of the 20th century was the large number of tea and coffee shops. The coffee shops were well patronised by the many cycling and touring clubs of the time. These two sketches are taken from a late-Victorian cycling magazine and show the Albany Coffee & Dining Rooms alongside the entrance to St John's church, and the Bay Tree Coffee House adjoining the *George Hotel*, and run by Mr. Ambrose Shaw.

49. An important occasion in the church calendar was the annual Sunday School outing.

50. Edwardian society as a whole was patriarchal and authoritarian. The local gentry represented authority and between them owned much of the land in and around Crawley in the years before the Great War. All that most people would see of the great landed estates would be the gates and lodges alongside. This photograph is of the South Lodge to the Crabbet Park Estate, which before 1916 spread out to the east of Crawley, and centred on the parish of Worth.

51. The Crabbet Estate originated in the late Middle Ages, but figures prominently in Crawley's history from 1698, when it was purchased by Leonard Gale Jr., son of the famous Sussex ironmaster, who made his home in the old Priest's House in Crawley High Street. Through the marriage of Sarah Gale in 1750, the estate passed to the Blunt family, and on the death of Francis Scawen Blunt in 1872, to his brother Wilfrid, who demolished the old manor house, replacing it in 1873 with a house, designed largely by Blunt's wife, Lady Anne, on late 17th-century lines.

52. Not far from Crabbet Park, to the east of Crawley, there lay the equally extensive Worth Park Estate, home of Sir Francis Montefiore. Unlike the simple classic lines of Crabbet Park House, the Worth Park mansion was built in the 1860s in an extravagant and lavish style, with the spacious terrace leading on to sweeping lawns and ornamental gardens.

53. The Hon. Mrs. Judith Anne Dorothea Blunt-Lytton, later 16th Baroness Wentworth, daughter and only surviving child of Wilfrid and Lady Anne Blunt. In his desire to ensure his daughter's inheritance of the family estates, Blunt in 1904 passed over the Crabbet Park Estate to Judith (who had married Neville Lytton in 1899). Retaining the name of Blunt, Judith and her family moved into Crabbet Park House in 1907.

54. & 55. Worth Park House reveals a mixture of styles. Whilst the exterior was built to a pseudo-Jacobean design, the state rooms were reminiscent of a later age, as can be seen here in these photographs of the dining room and billiard room. At Crabbet, Lady Wentworth excelled at billiards even in her eighties, easily beating Canadian troops billeted on her during the Second World War.

56. While celebration of royal occasions in Crawley was regular, royal visits were rare, so that the visit of Princess Alexander of Teck in July 1908 brought out the flags, bands and most of the population.

57. The great issues of the day made little impact on Crawley society, but in 1910 two general elections took place in one year following a constitutional crisis in the Houses of Parliament. Despite considerable national sympathy for the Liberal cause, and admiration for the Welsh firebrand, David Lloyd-George, the Horsham constituency, of which Crawley was a part, remained staunchly Conservative and on both occasions returned Earl Winterton as its parliamentary representative. This photograph shows the declaration of the poll from the balcony of the *Railway Hotel*.

58. During the constitutional crisis over the Parliament Bill, and in between elections, Edward VII died on 6 May 1910; Crawley turned out in force 10 days later on the occasion of his funeral to mourn a respected and well-loved king who, it was thought, had helped preserve peace in Europe.

CRAWLEY
TEMPERANCE
SOCIETY

Part Two: 1914–39

59. In both the political and social history of modern Britain, the outbreak of the First World War in August 1914 cannot be overestimated. Although Edward VII was king throughout the first decade of the 20th century, his reign was predominately Victorian. Edwardian Britain held hard to 19th-century principles. This changed with the outbreak of war, and the 20th century was born on the battlefields of France and Belgium in spirit if not in name. One of the first local men to join the colours was the Hon. Neville Lytton of Crabbet Park, husband of Judith Blunt-Lytton, who was commissioned into a Sussex Regiment.

60. The call of war and the exhortation to serve King and Empire cut across the social classes, with young Tom Briggs of West Green serving in the line.

61. Men from the Queen's Royal West Surreys at camp at Pease Pottage, near Crawley, in September 1916.

PARTICULARS

Lot 1

(Coloured Pink on Plan)

On the Borders of Surrey and Sussex, just under 30 miles from London, and 22 miles from Brighton; one-and-a-half miles from the ancient Town of Crawley, and adjacent to Three Bridges Junction on the main London and Brighton Railway, is the well-known Domain of

WORTH PARK

extending to

132 a. 1 r. 36 p.

The Principal Approach is within a quarter of a mile of Three Bridges Junction, and a pair of massive Cast Iron Gates with Lamp Pillars gives access to the

FINELY-TIMBERED PARK

protected by a Brick and Slated Gabled

ENTRANCE LODGE

(forming Lot 7)

containing Four Bedrooms, Parlour, Kitchen and Offices, Outhouses and Garden.

A WINDING DRIVE

some half-a-mile in length, flanked on either side by an Avenue of Limes and Oaks and finely grown timber and shrubs, winds its way through a wood terminating by a bold gravel sweep at the east side of the important

MANSION

built about 32 years ago in the ITALIAN STYLE OF ARCHITECTURE of Red Brick and Stone Facing with Tiled Roof and delightfully seated on the edge of the ancient Worth Forest nearly 300 feet above sea level, surrounded by

62. Although by no means destroying it, the Great War severely shook the foundations of the Victorian class structure in a number of ways. In 1915, the vast Worth Park Estate was sold off at auction by the childless Sir Francis Montefiore. Such a sale did not just include the mansion and surrounding parkland, but also widely-scattered farms. In the case of the Montefiore estates the land reached Crawley High Street itself. Among the numerous lots up for sale in September 1915 was the original Crawley Manor House, or 'Tree House', home of the Smith family.

By Order of the Honorable Mrs. BLUNT LYTTON.

ON THE NORTHERN BORDER OF SUSSEX.

70 minutes from London in a favourite Residential District. In the Parishes of

WORTH, IFIELD & CHARLEWOOD.

Particulars and Conditions of Sale

OF 63

OUTLYING PORTIONS

OF THE

Crabbet Park Estate

COMPRISING

HAZELWICK, WOOLBOROUGH, PRIORS, SCALLOWS, BLACKWATER, LITTLE BLACKWATER, FROGSHOLE, WAKEHAM'S GREEN, LAYHOUSE, COPTHORNE, TINSLOWS FARMS,

With Farmhouses, Homesteads and Cottages.

A Charming Residential Property, "**HAYHEATH,**"

A small SPORTING ESTATE known as HEATHY GROUND,

VILLA RESIDENCE,

Ye Old Curiosity Shop, Crawley,

30 COTTAGES, SMITHY, BUILDER'S PREMISES,

Various Pieces of BUILDING AND ACCOMMODATION LAND,

SMALL HOLDINGS,

400 ACRES of heavily TIMBERED WOODLAND,

THE WHOLE COVERING AN AREA OF ABOUT

1635 ACRES.

To be Sold by Auction by

MESSRS. COBB

At the GEORGE HOTEL, CRAWLEY,

On WEDNESDAY, SEPTEMBER 20th, 1916, at 3 p.m. precisely,

In 52 convenient Lots.

Particulars and Conditions of Sale, with Plans and Views, can be obtained at the place of Sale; of the Solicitors, Messrs. BURGESS, TAYLOR & TRYON, 1, New Square, Lincoln's Inn, W.C.; and of Messrs. H. & R. L. COBB, Auctioneers and Surveyors, 61 & 62, Lincoln's Inn Fields, London, W.C., and Higham, near Rochester.

The Printing Company, Limited, 77, High Street, Rochester.

63. The following year, 1916, saw the break up of much of the Crabbet Park Estate. Although Wilfrid Blunt had passed on the Crabbet lands to his daughter Judith in 1904 to preserve her inheritance, she felt the need in the midst of war to sell off much of the surrounding farms and heathlands, keeping for herself the mansion house and immediate parkland, where she would continue to breed the famous Crabbet Arabian horses.

64. Included in the sumptuous Crabbet Park sale catalogue of 1916 was the medieval cottage known as 'Ridley's Corner', on the junction of the Balcombe and Copthorne Roads.

65. The same view today: the sale sign 'Welcome to Crabbet Park' in the distance speaks volumes about the social revolution of the last 70 years, when the meaning of 'Crabbet Park Estate' has totally changed.

66. & 67. One of the gems in the 1916 Crabbet Park sale catalogue was Woolborough Farm; unfortunately nothing remains of the site, long since built over in the New Town 'Northgate' housing estate.

LOT 11.

(Coloured Green on Plan).

THE COMPACT AND LEVEL HOLDING

KNOWN AS

"WOOLBOROUGH,"

Conveniently and pleasantly situate close to Lot 9, in a ring fence, well protected and sheltered from the North-East by "Long Copse," and admirably adapted for

A RESIDENTIAL HOLDING, A STOCK BREEDING OR DAIRY FARMING ESTABLISHMENT

amidst pleasant surroundings, and comprising:—

Picturesque Farmhouse, 2 Cottages & Homestead of Agricultural Buildings

TOGETHER WITH

138 Acres of Arable Land and 71 Acres of well-timbered and shaded Pastures and Cool Meadows,

WITH

TWO PIECES OF WOODLAND,

68. & 69. Peace, when it finally came in June 1919, with the signing of the Paris Peace Treaty, was celebrated with great enthusiasm. These two plates show part of Crawley's peace celebrations, with the local schoolchildren marching up the High Street on their way to Mr. Moses Nightingale's house 'Hazeldene' (now the 'Crawley Club'). The illuminated word 'Pax' or 'Peace' over the entrance summed up the hopes of everyone.

70. The years following the Peace saw the erection of numerous memorials, and practically every village, town and city in Britain subscribed to its War Memorial, recording the names of those who did not return. This photograph shows the unveiling of Crawley's War Memorial in front of the parish church of St John the Baptist in 1920.

ARMISTICE PARADE AT CRAWLEY.

The Largest that has Yet been Held.

REPRESENTATIVE GATHERING.

71. (*below*) Crawley's other memorial to those local men who fell in the Great War was of a more practical and forward-looking nature. Although surrounded by fields, Crawley had no recreation ground until land was given in the 1920s for the use of the whole community. For many years, the 'rec' which lay just to the east of Crawley High Street along the Three Bridges Road was an open space, used by the local schools for games and sports. Surrounded today by shops, offices and busy roads, the old 'rec' has been landscaped and is known rather more formally as the Memorial Gardens—a welcome and peaceful oasis in what today is a busy, hectic town.

72. Similarly, the now weathered War Memorial still stands in front of St John's church; the dreams and aspirations of its architect and builder were not, however, to be entirely fulfilled and the names of the dead of another generation joined their fathers in 1945.

73. On the face of it, little had changed after the traumas of the Great War and life seemed to slip back comfortably into its old ways. Yet for Crawley as to the country as a whole signs of change were visible everywhere and before the decade was over the motor car had taken over from the horse-drawn vehicle as the main form of transport.

74. The advent of the motor vehicle confronted Crawley in a variety of ways in the 1920s. This photograph of about 1922, taken from Hoggs Hill, Southgate, looks northwards towards Crawley High Street, with the delivery cart of Hibbs the Bakers drawn up outside Hoggs Hill Farm. This is an interesting picture, showing two roads leading southwards out of Crawley: to the right is the original Brighton Road, while to the left a more negotiable thoroughfare has been cut into the side of the hill. Although a horse might be able to tackle a steep gradient, early gearboxes could not.

75. A pleasant view of Crawley parish church as seen from the east, along Three Bridges Road, in about 1925. This rural scene, which unfortunately no longer exists, remained comparatively unchanged for the next 30 years. It is today a busy, roaring dual carriageway, with only the church left as a distinctive landmark.

76. The popularity of motor travel in the 1920s and '30s resulted in roadside cafés springing up. Especially popular were the sedate 'Tea Shoppes' such as Ye Old Punche Bowle tea shop on Crawley Green. The building, dating from the 15th century, had been a farmhouse for generations and was then divided into cottages (*see* plate 3). The building was rescued from near dilapidation in the 1920s and restored to something of its former grandeur.

77. The years following the Great War saw a growing appreciation of vernacular historical buildings, with both the *George Hotel* and the Ancient Prior's House in Crawley High Street undergoing extensive restoration.

Visitors to CRAWLEY, who are looking for EARLY ENGLISH OAK, WALNUT and MAHOGANY FURNITURE, CHINA, GLASS and CURIOS should call at—

The Ancient Prior's House

This famous old Timber Framed Building, dating back seven centuries, is still in excellent condition and well worth a visit. On the main London to Brighton Road, opposite the old George Hotel.

J. W. PARKHURST
Proprietor.

78. While the rapidly-growing popularity of the motor car could hardly be ignored, there were other, more discreet indications that the world of 1914 had died with those whose names were on the new memorials. The rigid social structure of Victorian and Edwardian Britain had never fully recovered from the shocks of 1914-18. Following the sale and division of the Worth Park Estate in 1915, Sir Francis Montefiore's great mansion became a school for the daughters of Baptist ministers in the 1920s and was rechristened Milton Mount College.

79. Similarly, land which had once been part of Crawley's spacious estates was already being built on, such as Hazelwick Road, Three Bridges, seen in this postcard of the 1930s, with the Montefiore Institute to the right, a legacy of Sir Francis and a reminder of the patronage of a gradually-disappearing class of gentry.

80. (*above*) While much of Crabbet Park had been sold off in 1916, the mansion and surrounding parkland still remained the home and property of the Hon. Mrs. Judith Blunt-Lytton who, on the death of her mother in 1917, had become the 16th Baroness Wentworth. She was not as interested in administering a great estate as she was in breeding Arab horses. The 1920s and '30s saw the growth and world-wide fame of the Crabbet Arabian Stud and this photograph of about 1927 shows her with her horses and pet dog, seated in front of the Crabbet tennis court.

81. (*below*) Unlike the much larger Worth Park House, Crabbet Park House, designed and built in 1873, was to remain a private home, where Lady Wentworth lived until her death in 1957.

82. Crawley High Street in the 1920s, looking north from the railway station, a view which has changed little over the past 60 years.

34, HIGH STREET, CRAWLEY,

...AND AT...

. . . . . CHISLEHURST.

Telephone : 28 CRAWLEY.

PRICE ✦ LIST.

Madam,

We beg to submit to your notice our Daily Price list of Fish, Poultry and Game. All Goods warranted first-class quality at lowest possible prices.

A Trial Order is earnestly solicited, which shall receive personal attention.

Respectfully yours,

BASTABLE & SON.

P.T.O

83. Although the traditional social class structure was gradually changing, this was not as yet apparent to Crawley's tradesmen, who still sent boys on bicycles out to the kitchens of the 'big houses', and who themselves saw nothing amiss in leaving a shop full of customers to serve a distinguished lady, seated outside in her carriage, for whom to enter a shop and join a queue was unthinkable. In common with his tradesmen, the young Albert Bastable, when he arrived in Crawley in 1922 to manage his newly-acquired fish shop, was obliged to send out price lists, such as these: independence was still the prerogative of a few.

84. This would have been the first view of Crawley for the motorist driving into Crawley High Street from London in the 1920s and '30s. To the right of the photograph stands the *Sun Inn*, built in the 1860s, while opposite is the row known as 'Albert Cottages'.

85. The same view, photographed some 60 years later in 1986.

86. Such was the rapid development of the motor car in these inter-war years, that already by the 1930s the annual London to Brighton 'Old Crocks' rally was becoming a regular feature of Crawley life at a time when the High Street was still part of the main road (now known officially as the A23).

87. Along with the tea shops and roadside cafés, garages and petrol stations sprang up. One such establishment in Crawley was the Central Garage, aptly named since it stood in the middle of the High Street alongside the *George Hotel*. Like the Punche Bowle tea shop, the Central Garage building dated from the early Middle Ages yet, unlike its contemporary on the opposite side of the green, it has not survived and was demolished in the late 1930s for the construction of Grand Parade (*see* plate 116).

The Sussex Electricity Supply Company, Ltd.

CHEAPER ELECTRICITY

COOK BY ELECTRICITY.

On and after the June Quarter Meter Readings the Domestic Rate for Cooking and or Hot Water and or Refrigeration will be reduced to

2d. PER UNIT

88. Even long-established Crawley firms, like Ockendens the Undertakers of Ifield Road, were keeping up with the motor age; although greatly altered, this interesting building still stands in Ifield Road, opposite what until 1955 was West Green Church of England School (*see* plate 35).

89. Electricity had come to Crawley in 1909. The premises of the Southern Electricity Supply Co. were in Crawley Square, opposite the *George Hotel*.

90. The year 1928 saw the removal for the third time of one of Victorian Crawley's great institutions, the post office, back to the High Street. It had been exactly a century since William Mitchell took command of the village post office in 1828 in a house adjoining the *White Hart Inn* (*see* plate 152). Leaving its 1895 premises in Post Office Road (*see* plate 26), the Crawley post office took possession of this imposing mock-Queen Anne-style building, which was to dominate the southern end of the High Street, until its severe damage in the air raid of 1943 (*see* plate 124).

91. One of Crawley's long-established building firms, Bartley & Ward, with yard and clerical staff well-segregated, seen here in about 1923. Although the firm still survives, these buildings unfortunately do not, having been swallowed up by the dual carriageway which today links Crawley High Street with Haslett Avenue (*see* plates 146 & 147).

92. Mr. Bagley's Crawley Fish Stores, well prepared for a 1920s-style Christmas. The building was originally a 16th-century cottage at the junction of Crawley High Street with Ifield Road and, although severely damaged in a fire in 1983, it has been fully restored.

93. One of the happier legacies of the Great War was the formation of the Crawley Comrades Football Team, apparently successful at the close of the 1920-21 season.

94. Those too young to fight in 1914-18 were among the next generation to go to war in 1939. As yet oblivious of events in Europe, this class is working at Crawley Council School, Robinson Road, under the eagle eye of the woodwork master.

95. Although by the 1930s the wireless and the cinema were beginning to make their mark, entertainment was still predominantly 'home grown', especially with the likes of the Hazeldene Orchestra, which had first performed in the 1880s and was still thriving 50 years later. Moses Nightingale designed his villa, 'Hazeldene', with his orchestra in mind, as this photograph of his 'performance room' shows.

96. Moses and Ruth Nightingale at the time of their Golden Wedding Anniversary in 1934, an occasion which also marked the 50th anniversary of the orchestra's first performance.

97. The Victoria Hall was established in the 1920s at the northern end of Crawley High Street (*see* plate 140) for amateur dramatics and variety shows. On occasion, companies from London would perform, as this well-preserved ticket testifies.

98. A local variety troupe.

99. The cinema was regarded both as an exciting source of entertainment and as a useful means of information and communication. Crawley's first 'picture palace' was built just south of the railway line on Brighton Road in 1911. It became the Imperial cinema, but was burnt down in August 1928. A new Imperial was built on the same site later that year.

100. (*above*) It is easy to understand from these photographs of Crawley's Imperial cinema how 'going to the pictures' took people into a glamorous and exciting world before the film had even started to roll. This is the foyer and ticket office, with stairs leading to the balcony lounge, which had fashionable wicker chairs and chinese lanterns.

101. The interior of the Imperial. Today the ground floor is used as a car showroom and is totally changed, but the circle, used as a store room, still retains much of these original 1930s features, so beloved of early cinema architects.

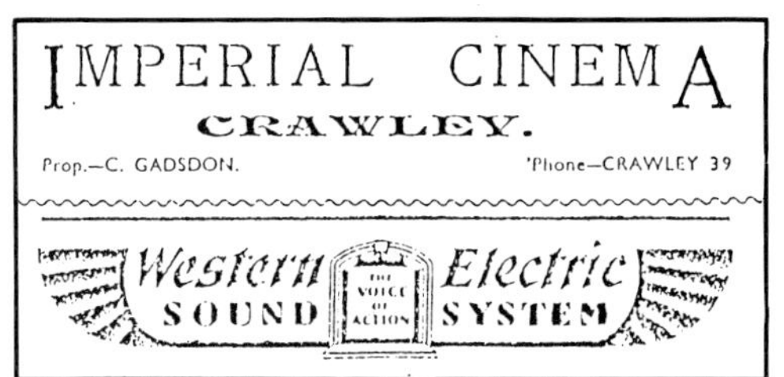

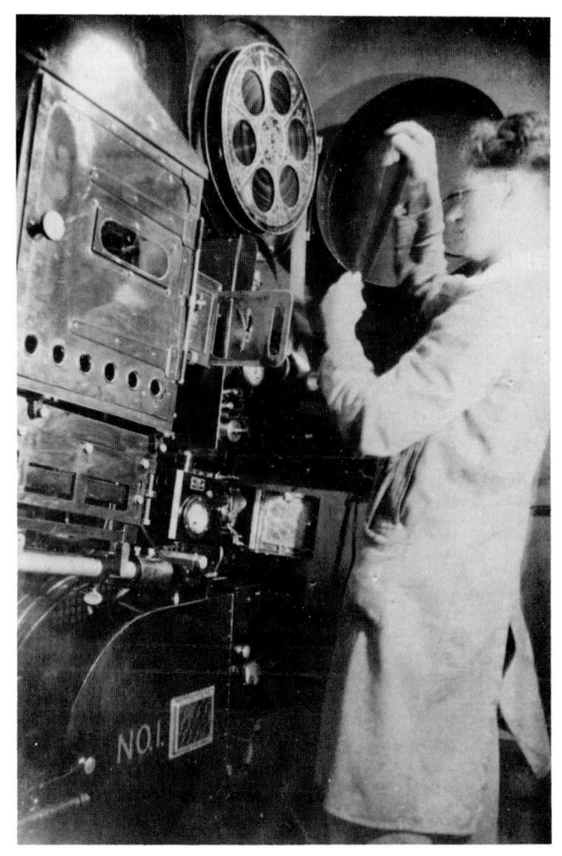

102. Imperial projectionist George Surridge.

103. The 'talkies' arrived at the beginning of the 1930s and, by contrast to the extravagant outpourings of Hollywood, inaugurated a more sober era on the political stage. Here, Prime Minister Ramsay MacDonald addresses a meeting on the platform of the Imperial.

104. The southern part of Crawley High Street on a Sunday morning in the mid-1930s. This area has changed comparatively little in 50 years, with the chemist shop still in business on the corner of what is now Station Way. To the right of the photograph can be seen the station approach and what for years must have been Crawley's smallest shop—The Cabin, tobacconist and sweet shop.

105. The approach led of course to the station itself, pictured here in about 1935. Built in 1848, when the London, Brighton & South Coast Railway Co. laid a branch line from Three Bridges to Horsham, Crawley railway station was a fine example of mid-Victorian railway architecture. It was unfortunately demolished in 1968 and as yet the site remains undeveloped, with a new, rather characterless station a few hundred yards further along the track.

106. & 107. George V had a special place in people's hearts probably because the 25 years of his reign had seen particularly difficult times, with the Great War and the subsequent economic depression of the early 1930s. Like the rest of Britain, Crawley was determined to celebrate the Silver Jubilee of this unassuming king, and in May 1935 the High Street was festooned with flags and bunting.

108. The reign of George V saw almost as many changes in Britain within 25 years as Victoria's had in over sixty. By the mid-1930s, it was becoming clear that the Great War had ushered in a new age, especially in travel. What, in 1930, was a small private airfield on the fringe of the village of Lowfield Heath to the north of Crawley had, by the middle of the decade, become Gatwick Aerodrome, with its terminal building, or 'Beehive' as it came to be known, built in 1936.

109. Gatwick Aerodrome (or airport as it was soon to be known) was the first in Britain to have its own railway station.

110. The popularity of the motor car grew steadily during the last years of the king's reign, with parking becoming a real problem; this photograph shows Crawley Square looking north, just after the George Annexe in the centre of the square had been demolished to provide more car parking space for hotel visitors. It was also at this time that AA patrols were placed at Crawley High Street's busy junctions, as can be seen to the extreme left, at the junction with Ifield Road—still a 'bottle-neck' 50 years later.

111. One of Crawley's best-known AA patrols was Mr. Bill Jacobs, seen here directing traffic on the Pound Hill crossroads.

112. A familiar sight even 50 years after this photograph was taken in Jubilee year, 1935. The Victorian engineers of the London, Brighton & South Coast Railway Co. could not have imagined the problems resulting nearly a century later, between the claims of the train and the motor car on the High Street. The traffic jams through Crawley High Street had become a serious problem by 1935, with cars and other vehicles queuing from the *Half Moon* at Southgate to the *Sun Inn* at Northgate. Britain's roads by the end of the Great War had changed little since the days of the tollgates and turnpikes and it was clear that a new road system had to be planned. Whereas the old roads had purposely passed through the towns and cities, the new network equipped for motor vehicles would need to avoid them, and a new word, 'bypass' slipped into the English language.

113. Just as, two centuries before, the road through Crawley was among the first to be turnpiked, so by the mid-1930s the proposed Crawley bypass was among the first in the country, and it was believed it would solve the town's chronic traffic hold-ups.

114. The widening of the road from Horsham into Crawley, with Buckswood Farm (now Cheal's Garden Centre) in the background.

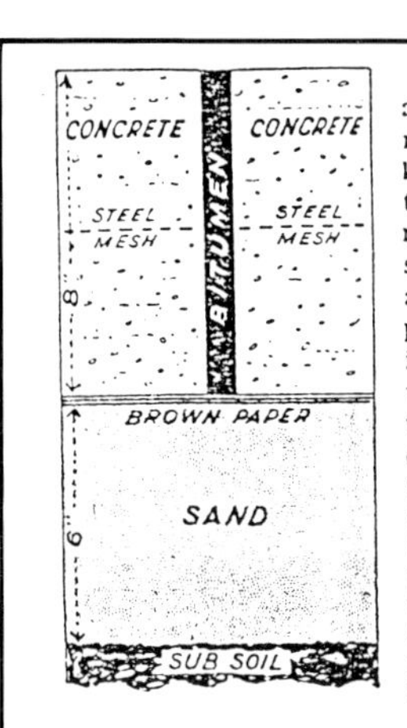

Simplicity and smoothness are the keynotes of the modern road. Cement, steel, sand, and brown paper—when it's all set it will stand up to a pressure of two tons to the square inch. And it takes a year to wear down the concrete even a paper's thickness.

Britain's newest road is laid on brown paper

115. Part of the Crawley bypass, shortly after its opening in 1939, and with that new phenomenon, the roundabout, in this case the junction of the new A23 with the A264 road leading to Horsham, again with Buckswood Farm in the distance. This view is much the same today, except that the farmland in the distance is now swallowed up by the Gossops Green residential estate, and that the roundabout is today as busy as Crawley High Street was half a century ago.

116. The 1930s made themselves felt also in two very distinctive buildings to the south of Crawley High Street, opposite the green. In a style rather reminiscent of London suburban shopping areas, and not dissimilar to the new post office (*see* plate 90) in its mock 18th-century design, Grand Parade, like the bypass, was only just completed by the outbreak of the Second World War in September 1939 and for the first years of its existence housed a number of rather dreary government offices, with the exception of Woolworth's, a colourful and exciting emporium where nothing cost more than a shilling.

117. By 1939, people were in no doubt that the world had irretrievably changed in the quarter of a century since war had been declared in August 1914. A few of the old landed estates still remained. One of Crawley's largest and most historic was the Tilgate Estate, to the south of Crawley, reminiscent not just of the heyday of the Victorian country estate, but even of the 17th-century ironworks and furnaces. From becoming a 'heavy' industrial area, Tilgate had crystalised into one of Crawley's sedate landed estates: as though to emphasise the extent of these estates, lodges at the foot of sweeping drives would appear periodically on Crawley's roads and lanes. This is the lodge and drive to Tilgate in Three Bridges High Street; the lodge house still stands today, as a branch of a bank.

SUSSEX

MIDWAY BETWEEN LONDON AND BRIGHTON.

Adjoining Three Bridges Junction. Three-quarters-of-a-mile from Crawley, twenty-one miles from Brighton and thirty-one miles from London.

Particulars, Plan, Views and Conditions of Sale of the

IMPORTANT FREEHOLD

Residential, Agricultural and Building Estate

KNOWN AS

Tilgate

Near CRAWLEY

Extending to about

2,185 Acres

including nearly 800 Acres of

Well-grown Mixed Woodlands and Plantations

a large area of

Valuable Building Land

and

A Substantial Mansion

THE ESTATE IS ALMOST TITHE FREE

VACANT POSSESSION OF PRACTICALLY THE WHOLE

For Sale by Auction as a whole or in blocks or Lots by Messrs.

KNIGHT, FRANK & RUTLEY

(W. Gibson, D.S.O., F.S.I., F.A.I.; G. M. Cannon; A. J. Baker, F.S.I., F.A.I.; M. Mackenzie (U.S.A.) and E. Fisher)

At the Montefiore Institute, Three Bridges

On THURSDAY the 7th day of SEPTEMBER, 1939

at 2 o'clock

(unless previously disposed of privately).

SOLICITORS : Messrs. ELVY ROBB & CO., 19, Bedford Row, W.C.1.

LAND AGENTS : Messrs. BERNARD THORPE & PARTNERS, 32, Millbank, Westminster, London, S.W.1. (Phone : Victoria 3012).

AUCTIONEERS : Messrs. KNIGHT, FRANK & RUTLEY, 20, HANOVER SQUARE, LONDON, W.1 (Phone : Mayfair 3771).

118. There can be few more poignant documents in Crawley's history than the sale catalogue of the Tilgate Estate, dated Thursday 7 September 1939, just four days after Britain's declaration of war on Hitler's Germany.

Part Three: 1940–52

119. (*above*) With the threat of German invasion in the summer of 1940, Crawley lay in the path of attack and, for once, its proximity to London appeared to be something of a liability. This is an early photograph of a local Home Guard platoon.

120. (*below*) This photograph shows the Crawley Home Guard marching down Crawley High Street in 1943, fully armed, in honour of their third birthday.

121. Expecting that Hitler would use the poisonous gas employed with such devastation during the Great War on civilian targets, everyone was issued with gas masks. The testing of gas masks was a regular occurrence in wartime Crawley, as in this photograph of 1943, showing a testing operation by a group of G.P.O. workers.

122. It was evident that once the 'Phoney War' of 1939-40 was over, civilian areas would be part of the 'front line'. Children were evacuated to Crawley from London and Canadian troops were billeted in Tilgate Park, Worth Park (by now Milton Mount) and Crabbet Park. Many socials and dances were held in the old *Railway Hotel* assembly rooms. This photograph shows Mrs. Longley's accordion band which was a tremendous morale booster during the war.

123. By contrast, a more sombre reminder of war came with the air raid of February 1943 which, among other things, demolished a good part of the post office in the High Street and totally destroyed Willett's stationers and printer's shop, from which many of Crawley's Edwardian postcards were published. Despite the devastation shown here, there were no fatalities in the High Street, although a number were killed in Station Road behind.

124. Men doing clearance work on the post office.

125. As no rebuilding could be attempted during wartime, the post office had to rely on temporary premises around the town, such as this tent in nearby Station Road.

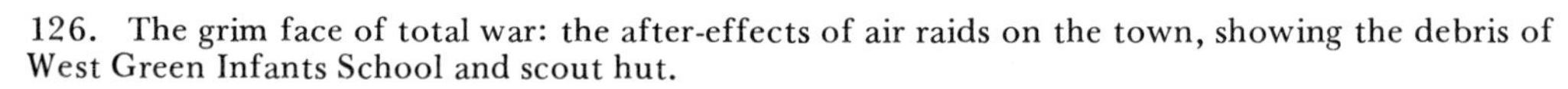
126. The grim face of total war: the after-effects of air raids on the town, showing the debris of West Green Infants School and scout hut.

127. (*above*) A number of houses in Station Road were totally destroyed.

128. (*below*) Perhaps the saddest 'building' casualty of German raids on Crawley was that of the Baptist church in Station Road, built in 1883. For 40 years after the war the church was Crawley's public library and then Crawley Boxing Club, before it was demolished with the whole of Station Road in 1985 to make way for redevelopment. A new Baptist church was opened in West Green in 1953.

CRAWLEY AND IFIELD

WINGS FOR VICTORY WEEK

JUNE 19th to 26th, 1943.

129. Despite the devastation and death that the 1943 air raids brought to Crawley, a growing sense of victory was felt and in the summer of that year a successful 'Wings for Victory' week was held, with a march past in Crawley High Street in front of the Canadian Governor-General on the flag-bedecked dais.

130. The end of the Second World War ushered in an era of social change and upheaval far greater than that of 1919; perhaps the clearest indication of changes ahead came with the rejection of Winston Churchill and the election of a Labour government in July 1945, armed with a radical social programme. Despite this, the months immediately following the end of the war saw Crawley 'picking up the pieces' and resuming its role as a small country town. A sure indication that life was returning to normal was the demolition of the air raid shelter in front of the *George Hotel* in 1946.

131. (*above*) For those demobilised in 1946 and 1947 Crawley seemed not to have changed since their childhood, surrounded by fields and woods. This is an interesting photograph taken from the roof of the Embassy cinema in the late 1940s, looking north towards London. The land to the immediate north of the cinema has now been built on by Sussex House and the bowling alley.

132. (*below left*) A fascinating photograph taken in 1945 as part of the peace celebration, showing the Punch Bowle tea shop. The people seen here in Victorian period dress are members of some of Crawley's oldest families including Mrs. Marigold Crowe and Miss Florrie Warren, both High Street traders.

133. (*below right*) In 1945 Judith, Lady Wentworth, still lived on at Crabbet Park. Although in her seventies when this photograph was taken, she retained much of her famed beauty. A brilliant horsewoman, Lady Wentworth published her most famous work *The Authentic Arabian Horse and His Descendants* in 1945.

134. While central Europe lay shattered, Crawley in the late 1940s remained much as it had for years. This photograph taken in the early 1950s shows one of Crawley's oldest thoroughfares, the junction of the High Street with Woolborough Lane, with the gasometer and Victorian Gasworks Cottages in the background.

135. By the early 1950s it was clear that Crawley was on the brink of momentous change. The same view in 1986: while the roads are still there, the aura of a small country town has gone.

136. *(above)* A view of Three Bridges Road taken in the early 1950s from the corner of Station Road, showing a row of substantial 1930s 'mock-Tudor' houses behind St John's church, and backing on to Crawley Tennis and Bowling Club.

137. *(below)* The same view in 1986, illustrating the changes Crawley has experienced since becoming a New Town.

138. The area to the north of Crawley High Street known as Northgate, seen here in about 1950. This was where the North Toll-gate crossed the street when the Crawley turnpike lay on the coaching route from London to Brighton in the 18th and 19th centuries. By the time that this photograph was taken, the building to the left had become the Northgate Restaurant, but it was originally the *Rising Sun*, one of Crawley's famous coaching inns.

139. The same view in 1986 shows only the late medieval house known as 'Boscobel' remaining. Despite the erection of offices on this site over the past decade, great effort has been made to lend character to the area, and the greatly-restored 'Boscobel' does not appear at all out of place.

140. To the left of the Northgate Restaurant in 1950 there stood what once had been the Victoria Hall, but which by this time had become the premises of a light engineering works. To the left can be seen the garage for the London Transport Bus Co., which has recently been demolished.

141. The same view today shows only what was the petrol station on the corner of Northgate Road remaining, and even that boarded up.

142. By the late 1940s what had earlier been the home of Crawley's postmaster, Charles Mitchell, was now the tobacconist and confectioner's shop of Mrs. Frances Hogger, in Robinson Road. It was Mrs. Hogger who had organised one of Crawley's many V.E. Day parties. Facing Crawley Council School (previously the British School), Mrs. Hogger's shop was one of the most popular and best patronised in Crawley.

143. One Crawley couple especially relieved to see the safe demobilisation of their three sons from the forces were the author's grandparents, Mr. and Mrs. Albert Bastable. Albert first came to Crawley in 1922, shortly after his demobilisation from the army in the Great War. For the next 60 years, his fish shop in the High Street was well known, with his wife, Violet, establishing the fried fish side of the business during the Second World War. By the 1980s, Albert Bastable had become Crawley's oldest tradesman and as much an institution as any building, working in his shop less than two months before his death in February 1986, at the age of 86.

144. The Square, Crawley High Street, in the early 1950s. This was still the centre of the town's shopping community, with the distinctive block of shops in the middle of the street facing the church.

145. Despite the dominance of Grand Parade, which was completed after the war, Crawley High Street in the early 1950s still captured the atmosphere of a country town, although by this time work was progressing on the development of the New Town.

146. The junction of Three Bridges Road and Crawley High Street. By this time some of the shops were part of Crawley's 'Co-operative' stores, with different departments occupying premises scattered around the High Street, until the new store was opened in Queen's Square in 1957.

147. Exactly the same view in 1986; to the right can be seen the side of the old post office, largely rebuilt after the air raid of 1943. The post office moved to new premises in the Boulevard in 1959.

148. Among the first of Crawley High Street's old buildings to be demolished for the New Town was this interesting row of tiny cottages along Crawley Green and in front of which, many years before, the stalls and sideshows of the Crawley Fair were set up.

149. Much the same view, 33 years later in 1986, after the cottages and houses between the *Brewery Shades* and *White Hart* had been pulled down to link the High Street with the new shopping centre, and the first stage of central Crawley's development—the Broadwalk.

150. Apart from the houses and cottages which fronted on to the High Street, a considerable amount of land had to be cleared behind, on which had stood for over 150 years the extensive stables of the *White Hart Inn*, built in 1790, in order to cope with Crawley's great volume of traffic. By 1953, when this photograph was taken, they had become garages, serving the needs of a later generation.

151. The same view in 1986, with the Broadwalk providing a pedestrianised link between the old and new towns.

152. One of the buildings alongside the *White Hart* which was demolished in 1953 was the early 19th-century house, which in 1828 became Crawley's post office with William Mitchell in charge. In later years, after the post office's move to Post Office Road (now Robinson Road) it became a sweet shop, which it remained until its demolition.

153. The same view in 1986, with the approach to Cross Keys and Herbert's Sports Shop standing on its site.

154. The second link between the High Street and the new shopping centre was to be the Boulevard, to run parallel with what had once been the private driveway to Crawley Rectory. This photograph, again dating from the early 1950s, shows the new roadway being prepared, with two of Crawley's oldest buildings, the Tree House and the Punch Bowle (by now a branch of the National Provincial Bank) on either side.

155. The same view in 1986, from the steps of the Embassy cinema. The junction between the High Street and the Boulevard is today one of the busiest and noisiest in Crawley.

156. Shops in the centre of Crawley High Street, boarded up and awaiting demolition in 1957.

157. The same view in 1986; the High Street has been robbed of a good deal of its character.

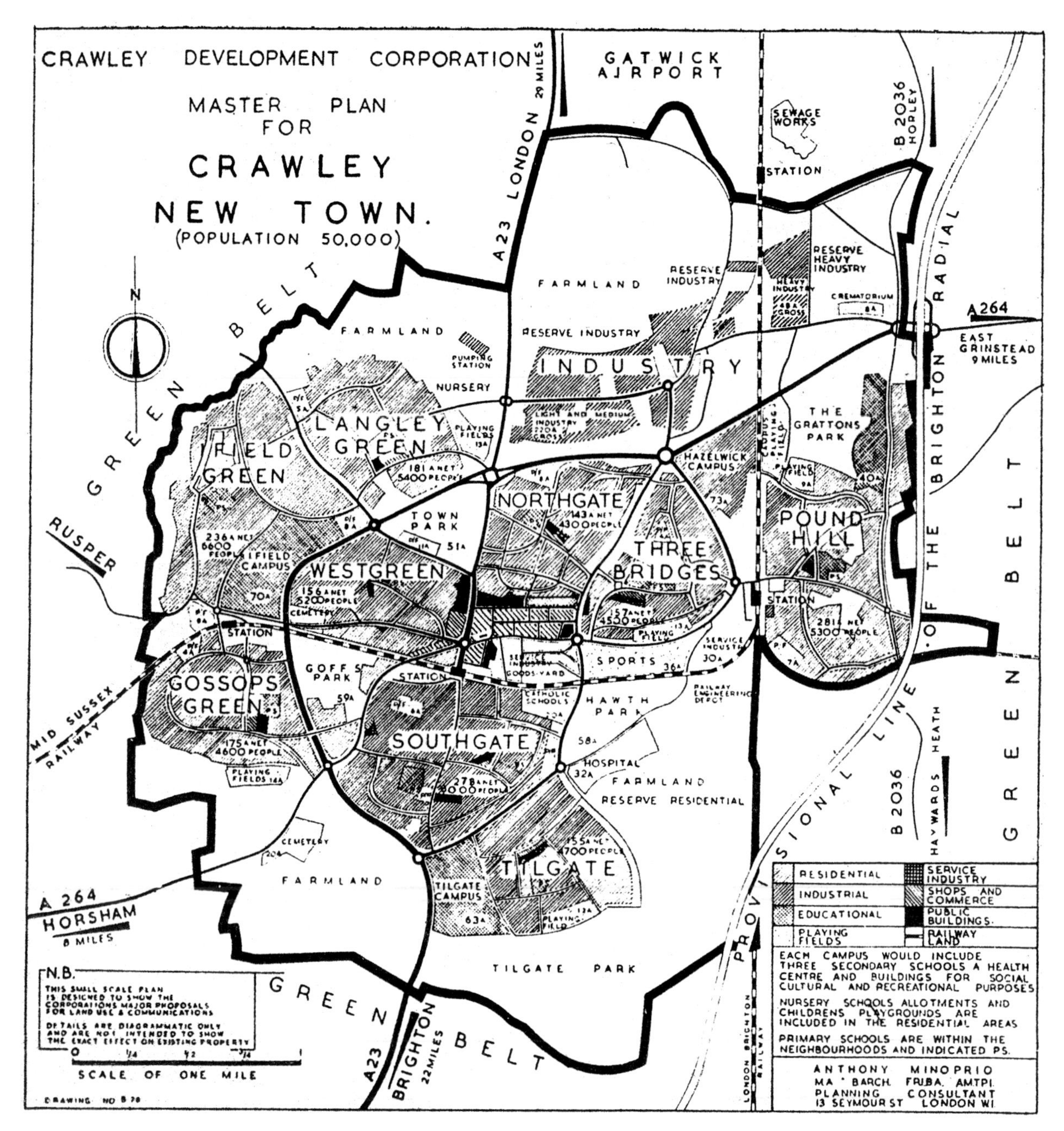

158. & 159. (*above & opposite*) The radical plans of the new Labour government hit Crawley more than a year after V.E. Day, with the announcement that it had been designated one of the first new 'satellite' towns to be built around London. The idea of purpose-built New Towns was not a recent one, but it had never been put into operation on quite the scale envisaged by the Ministry of Town and Country Planning and the newly set-up Development Corporations. Seemingly endless discussion and planning took place in the closing years of the 1940s until, in 1949, work started on the new Industrial Estate on farmland to the north of Crawley at County Oak, and the first housing estates. The photograph opposite (plate 159) shows the laying of the main road to the Industrial Estate.

160. (*below*) The completed road some months later, with the old London Road in the distance.

161. A significant day in the history of Crawley New Town came on 25 January 1950, with the visit to Crawley of H.R.H. Princess Elizabeth; while Crawley's designation as a New Town had taken place back in 1947, it was the Princess's visit three years later which seemed properly to inaugurate the start of a scheme unparalleled in Crawley's thousand-year history. Here the Princess cuts the ribbon to open the main roadway to what was to become known from now on as the Manor Royal Industrial Estate. Within a short time factories were to be built, and workers and their families moved from London into the new houses on the neighbourhood estates.

162. Following the official opening of the Manor Royal, Princess Elizabeth was driven into Crawley High Street, as yet untouched by New Town development. She planted a tree on Crawley Green to commemorate the billeting of Canadian forces to the town during the war. This was to be the first of three visits she has made to Crawley.

163. The chairman of Crawley Parish Council who had the honour of accompanying the Princess around Crawley on that day was Mr. Percy Wales, a local businessman and 'old towner', who, with his colleagues including Miss Daisy Warren, saw that the interests of an already long-established town were not overlooked in the construction of the new.

164. Within a short period of time, the burgeoning Crawley New Town was to become something of a national show-piece, with Mr. Wales appearing on BBC television.

165. An interesting panorama of Crawley as seen from the tower of St John's church in about 1950, with the High Street and traditional buildings of the *George Hotel* and Ancient Prior's in the foreground, while beyond, in what for centuries had been farmland, the new Crawley, in this case the West Green housing estate, was growing.

166. One of the first roads of Crawley New Town's first neighbourhood estate of West Green was Smalls Mead, shown here in the course of construction in 1949. It was appropriate that this should be the first of Crawley's new neighbourhood areas since in many ways West Green was as old as Crawley itself, with a medieval community gathered around the village green, on which St Peter's church was built in 1892.

167. One of the first London firms to bring their work-force down to Crawley from Wandsworth was the A.P.V. Co. This early photograph of about 1954 shows some of the staff outside the new works office.

168. Old Jordans Farm at County Oak was to become the A.P.V. Social Club. This couple jiving to one of the new exciting Rock'n'Roll records of the mid-1950s shows that Crawley had well and truly entered a new era by 1956.

169. For families who had only been used to rented rooms in London, the prospect of a new house and new life in Crawley was a dream come true. Here a young family look with excitement at the progress of their new home. 'I remember at our interview with the Housing Authority we were asked which type of house we would like, and were given a book with different designs and styles to choose from—after living in three rooms with two young children, it was all a bit overwhelming.'

170. An entirely new phenomenon in the planning of the West Green estate was the construction of low flats, built just behind the Embassy cinema.

171. The plans: the architect's model for new housing in West Green.

172. The reality: a young family clearly well pleased with their new home in West Green.

Part Four: 1953–86

173. & 174. Crawley Carnival 1953. The annual Whit Monday procession wends its way through the High Street along by the *White Hart* and the *Railway Hotel*.

175. By 1953, Crawley was participating in a development unparalleled in its colourful past; by the year that Queen Elizabeth II was crowned, the first neighbourhood estates were, amongst the mud and building sites, beginning to find their identity. This photograph of the Langley Green Carnival in the early 1950s gives some idea of the growing sense of community.

176. The architect's model for the new Crawley shopping centre. In contrast to the traditional High Street, thronged with traffic, the trend for the 1950s and '60s was for the shops to be built around a large square.

177. The official opening of the Broadwalk in 1954 by the Conservative Minister of Housing and Local Government, Mr. Duncan Sandys. To his left stands the chairman of Crawley Development Corporation, Sir Thomas Bennett.

178. Sir Thomas had an even more distinguished guest four years later, when the Queen made a return visit to Crawley on 9 June 1958 to open the new Gatwick Airport. Having visited the newly completed area, appropriately christened Queen's Square, Her Majesty walked through the Broadwalk and out into Crawley High Street on her way to lunch at the *George Hotel*, as she had eight years before, and as at least one of her illustrious predecessors (George IV) had many times before that.

179. Once the Broadwalk had been completed in 1954 work began on the main shopping precinct. This photograph of about 1956 shows the eastern end of the Broadwalk and the construction of what was to be the new Co-operative Store.

180. Thirty years later, and what has now become a well-established part of central Crawley.

181. It was envisaged in the early 1950s that each neighbourhood unit would remain as independent as possible, with its own shops, schools, church and public house. This was a fair enough assumption 30 years ago, when many married women did not go out to work and few families owned cars. Thus, despite new buildings, the nature of the shops on the estate 'shopping parade' was traditional, including bakers, greengrocers, and butchers. This is a plan for the Northgate estate.

182. Reality followed on rapidly from the models and plans and, by the early years of the 1950s, Northgate, Crawley's second neighbourhood estate, began to rise up from what were once fields to the north-east of the High Street. This photograph shows construction work around the shopping and community area of Northgate as seen in the model above.

183. (*above*) The Three Bridges estate was built soon after Northgate, like West Green around an already existing community—the small railway town to the east of Crawley. This was to lead to the amalgamation of Crawley and Three Bridges. This interesting photograph records the dedication of the new church of Three Bridges by the much-loved Bishop George Bell of Chichester, who also gave his name to one of Crawley's new junior schools, Bishop Bell School in Tilgate. The church at Three Bridges was appropriately dedicated to St Richard of Chichester.

184. (*below*)The Anglican and Catholic churches in Crawley co-operated with the local authorities in the planning and building of new schools for the neighbourhood estates. The coming of the New Town and the 1944 Education Act meant that Crawley's traditional schools were out of date. The town's oldest school, West Green Church of England School (originally Sarah Robinson's National School), was closed in 1955, with pupils moving to the new St Margaret's Church of England School further along Ifield Road, seen here during construction in 1954.

185. One of the first classes to join St Margaret's School in September 1955, seen here five years later in 1960. As in many of the junior schools in Crawley at this time, classes were a mixture of children who were new to the town and those whose families had been part of Crawley for generations. The author is at the back row to the extreme left.

186. A younger class at Northgate Junior (now Middle) School at about the same time. It is interesting to compare these two photographs with those of a previous Crawley generation (*see* plates 29, 37 & 38).

187. These cottages, older than their brick fronts suggest, were the last to remain in Crawley High Street, until they were demolished in 1965.

188. The same view in 1986.

189. Station Road had a short but interesting life. The road can be traced in the 1870 map at the beginning of this book, although no buildings were marked. Station Road developed as Crawley's population increased in the 1870s and '80s. This photograph was taken in 1984, when the houses to the right were being demolished for office development. To the left can be seen Crawley's first police station (1883).

190. By 1986 nothing of the old Station Road remains.

Plates 191 to 194 were all taken in the summer of 1986. They should be compared with earlier plates, details of which are given in the captions, to show how Crawley has developed during the last 100 years.

191. (*see* plate 4) This part of the town has altered beyond recognition over the past 100 years; most of the buildings in plate 4 no longer exist.

192. Surprisingly little has changed in this area during the last century (*see* plate 11). Building has extended along the Brighton Road on the other side of the railway line, but the dominating feature of both photographs is the railway signal box. Such a vital part of operations in 1886, the box was closed and boarded up in the early summer of 1986, and its future remains uncertain, although hopes are high for its preservation. Perhaps the most surprising thing to note from these two photographs is not what has changed but what has remained; it would have startled many, including the early town planners, to see that after nearly 140 years traffic in Crawley High Street is still brought to a standstill by the regular passage of trains.

193. When compared with plate 12, this is a sad photograph, with the old station and platforms demolished and fenced off, and only the *Rocket* and boarded-up signal box as a reminder of Crawley's railway history. The *Railway Hotel* assembly rooms to the left of plate 12, scene of many Victorian concert parties organised by Mark Lemon, and dances for the Canadian troops in the 1940s, were destroyed by fire in 1966.

194. (*see* plate 16) Station Road, seen here in 1986, has known exceptional change even for Crawley. The Victorian street which had been badly damaged at this southern end in 1943 was entirely demolished in 1985-86, and the construction of offices is well under way, although as yet incomplete.

195. There are many reminders of the social and economic changes which have taken place not just in Crawley, but in Britain as a whole, over the last century. Perhaps the most indicative is the complete disappearance of those country estates which until the Great War of 1914-18 encircled Crawley. Their disappearance ushered in an entirely different social order. Where the once grand mansion of Worth Park House stood (plate 52) there is today a block of flats, following the demolition of the 'big house', which had latterly become Milton Mount School for Girls (plate 79).

196. Despite the rather uniform and bland architecture of the flats in comparison with the exotic design of the original mansion, the surrounding terraces and gardens have been well preserved and it is still possible to recapture the feeling of the Victorian country estate.

197. One by one Crawley's great estates were sold and divided off. While on the death of Lady Wentworth in 1957, the Crabbet Arabian Stud continued, other parts of the Crabbet Park estate itself were sold off. Ironically the cutting through the old parkland of the M23 motorway in the early 1970s made the area desirable and popular because of its close proximity to London and Gatwick Airport. During the latter part of the 1970s, the Crabbet Park Housing Estate was built, with the main driveway to the old estate becoming Wentworth Drive, the main road to the new housing estate.

198. Fortunately, unlike Worth Park House or Tilgate Park House, Crabbet Park House has survived. It first became a boys' school and was subsequently divided off into flats. In the early 1980s the house was sold to a development company which had it extensively restored and refurbished for use as luxury offices. While most of the rooms were adapted as modern offices, the grand entrance hall and ground floor rooms were restored and renovated to look much as they must have done when the house was built in 1873. This photograph, taken in the winter of 1984/85, shows Crabbet Park House just after restoration work was completed and shortly before its occupation by a computer company, which has taken pains to preserve the building's historic character.

199. The dilapidated remains of Lady Wentworth's tennis court and swimming pool at Crabbet Park in 1985. It was here that she had been photographed with her Arab horses. Fortunately the building is about to be restored and renovated.

200. In 1986 Crawley looks forward to the 40th anniversary of its designation as a New Town. In anticipation of this, the Crawley Festival was held in and around the town from 15 to 21 June 1986, the centre of which was a nightly *Son et Lumière* production showing Crawley's colourful history from its Anglo-Saxon and Norman origins, with St John's church (founded 1250) as a suitable backdrop for the unfolding of a unique story. This photograph shows the stage and arena alongside the church, in readiness for the final performance.

201. An historic event for Crawley was the closing of the High Street on Saturday 21 June 1986 for the first time in over 60 years, for the return of the Crawley High Street Fair, which had been part of local life and tradition since the days of King John until its abolition in the 1920s. Crawley has often been unfairly dubbed a 'faceless New Town', so the festival set out to remind the town's 80,000 inhabitants that it has roots set deep in British history. Whether the 1986 High Street midsummer fair marks the restoration of a centuries-old Crawley tradition, only time will tell.